by Victor Gentle and Janet Perry

Gareth Stevens Publishing
A WORLD ALMANAC EDUCATION GROUP COMPANY

Please visit our web site at: www.garethstevens.com
For a free color catalog describing Gareth Stevens Publishing's
list of high-quality books and multimedia programs,
call 1-800-542-2595 or fax your request to (414) 332-3567.

Library of Congress Cataloging-in-Publication Data

Gentle, Victor.
    Cheetahs / by Victor Gentle and Janet Perry.
        p. cm. — (Big cats: an imagination library series)
    Includes bibliographical references and index.
    Summary: An introduction to the physical characteristics, behavior, natural environment,
and threats to the survival of the cheetah, considered to be the fastest land animal on Earth.
    ISBN 0-8368-3024-5 (lib. bdg.)
    1. Cheetah—Juvenile literature. [1. Cheetah. 2. Endangered species.] I. Perry, Janet, 1960-
II. Title.
QL737.C23G46   2002
599.75'9—dc21   2001049692

First published in 2002 by
Gareth Stevens Publishing
A World Almanac Education Group Company
330 West Olive Street, Suite 100
Milwaukee, WI 53212 USA

Text: Victor Gentle and Janet Perry
Page layout: Victor Gentle, Janet Perry, and Tammy Gruenewald
Cover design: Tammy Gruenewald
Series editor: Catherine Gardner
Picture Researcher: Diane Laska-Swanke

Photo credits: Cover, pp. 9, 11, 13 © Alan & Sandy Carey; pp. 5, 15, 19, 21
© Anup Shah/BBC Natural History Unit; p. 7 © Fritz Pölking/Visuals Unlimited;
p. 17 © Simon King/BBC Natural History Unit

Printed in the United States of America

1 2 3 4 5 6 7 8 9 06 05 04 03 02

Front cover: On the plains of Kenya in East
Africa, three members of a family of cheetahs
bathe in the rays of the setting Sun.

TABLE OF CONTENTS

Words that appear in the glossary are printed in **boldface** type the first time they occur in the text.

FASTER THAN A SPEEDING...

Cheetahs are the fastest animals that live on land. How fast can they really go? At top speed, cheetahs run as fast as 70 miles (113 kilometers) per hour. Scientists disagree about exact speeds.

The fastest humans run about 23 miles (37 km) per hour. Greyhounds race at 39 miles (63 km) per hour. **Gazelles** reach 50 miles (80 km) per hour.

Cheetahs run as fast as cars travel on a highway. They are fast, but they cannot run at top speed for long. If they try that, cheetahs get too hot and run out of breath.

Cheetahs can run at top speed for about ten seconds. If an animal stays ahead of the cheetah for longer than that, it will probably escape.

BUILT FOR SPEED

Cats are built for running, slinking, springing, and climbing. Some cats are better at one thing than another. Cheetahs are best at running fast.

Cheetahs can run fast because they have sleek bodies and light bones. They also have long legs and a bendy spine, which let them take very long running steps. As cheetahs run, their paws grip the ground with claws, like running shoes with spikes. Cheetahs pant hard through extra-wide nostrils to catch their breath and cool down.

Cheetahs must turn fast at top speed. Their **prey**, like this hare, often zigzags to escape. Long tails help cheetahs zigzag tightly to keep up.

FAST FOOD

Like all cats, cheetahs eat only meat. So, they eat other animals for food. Cheetahs hunt birds, hares, **gnus**, **warthogs**, and young zebras and wildebeests. Cheetahs are champions at catching gazelles in open grasslands with few trees.

Gazelles are fast, deerlike animals. They can run faster over longer distances than cheetahs can. If a cheetah starts close to a gazelle, it can speed up fast enough to catch the gazelle.

A cheetah chases its favorite food — a Thomson's gazelle. Fast food must be eaten fast, too, before other **predators** arrive.

EATING ON THE RUN

The chase is on. At top speed, the cheetah twists and turns behind the gazelle. With a swipe of its paw, the cheetah topples the gazelle, bites into its neck, and kills it.

The cheetah has just enough strength left to eat. It is too tired to fight off other predators. The cheetah gobbles its food before slower-moving meat eaters, like hyenas, vultures, jackals, leopards, or lions, can get there and steal its meal. Lions might even attack and·eat the cheetah!

Here, a cheetah family eats fast. Cheetahs never **scavenge**. They are such good hunters, they do not have to.

CHEETAHS IN DANGER

Every day, cheetahs are in danger from predators and people. People are the biggest threat. In fact, people might wipe out all cheetahs.

People kill cheetahs for sport, for skins, and sometimes to protect farm animals. People build farms and factories in the wild, open spaces that cheetahs need to live and hunt. People kill the animals that cheetahs count on for food. Diseases from farm dogs might make cheetahs very sick.

In most countries, it is illegal to hunt cheetahs or to sell their beautiful, black-spotted, pale yellow skins. **Poaching** is still a big problem.

ON THE EDGE AGAIN

Cheetahs were nearly **extinct** once before. About 10,000 years ago, most cheetahs died. Nobody knows why so many died at one time. All today's cheetahs come from the few survivors. So, all cheetahs are almost exactly alike.

Humans are better off than cheetahs because we are so different from each other. A deadly disease might kill some of us, but not all of us. Cheetahs, however, are *too alike*. If a disease comes along that kills one cheetah, then the disease would probably kill all the cheetahs.

Only a hundred years ago, cheetahs lived in Asia, the Middle East, and Africa. Now, most remaining cheetahs live south of the Sahara Desert in Africa.

ALONE OR TOGETHER?

Many male cheetahs live in groups of two, three, or sometimes four. They mark an area of land called a **territory**. If other males enter their territory, they will fight them — or even kill them.

Female cheetahs live alone. They do not defend territories. Females share their hunting land with other cheetahs, but they stay away from each other.

Male and female cheetahs get together to **mate**. About three months later, the female gives birth to **cubs**. One to eight cubs are born in a **litter**.

These cheetahs look out across the East African plains. No doubt, they are thinking about supper.

BRINGING UP BABIES

Life is hard for cheetah cubs. Other predators, even another cheetah, might kill them. The father does not help raise the cubs.

The mother works hard to protect her cubs from predators. When she goes hunting, she hides the cubs in long grass. She moves them to new hiding places often.

For six weeks, the cubs drink only their mother's milk. Then, they follow her and eat at her kills, too. After three months, the cubs eat only meat.

Newborn cubs are as light as a can full of soda pop. As adults, cheetahs are about as long (and as heavy) as two dalmatians standing head to tail.

WILL CHEETAHS SURVIVE?

Young cheetahs play hard to learn the skills for hunting. Then, sometime after their first birthday, they leave their mother.

Will they know how to escape danger on their own? Will they be shot by farmers protecting their cattle? Will they die because rich people want to own cheetah skins? Will a disease wipe them out? Or will people who care about cheetahs be able to protect them?

For cheetahs, the future is terribly uncertain.

In the wild, cheetahs may live 12 to 14 years. But only one of every three cubs will grow up. Humans cut short the lives of many cheetahs.

MORE TO READ AND VIEW

Books (Nonfiction)
    Big Cats (series). Victor Gentle and Janet Perry (Gareth Stevens)
    Blanca and Arusha. Georgeanne Irvine (Simon and Schuster)
    How It Was with Dooms. Xan Hopcraft and Carol Cawthra Hopcraft
      (Margaret McElderry)
    The Living World. Record Breakers (series). David Lambert
      (Gareth Stevens)
    Pippa, the Cheetah, and Her Cubs. Joy Adamson (Harcourt & World)
    Quick and Slow Animals. Barbara J. Behm (Gareth Stevens)
    What Do We Know about Grasslands? Brian Knapp (Peter Bedrick)
    What's Faster than a Speeding Cheetah? Robert E. Wells (Whitman)
    Who Knows This Nose? Marlene M. Robinson (Dodd, Mead)

Books (Activity)
    Drawing the Big Cats. Paul Frame (Franklin Watts)

Videos (Nonfiction)
    Animal Disguises. Amazing Animals (series). (Dorling Kindersley)
    Maximum Cheetah Velocity. Kratt's Creatures (series). (PolyGram Video)
    Running Out of Time. (Kurtis Productions: WTTW)
    Swinging Safari. Really Wild Animals (series). (Columbia TriStar)

PLACES TO VISIT, WRITE, OR CALL

Cheetahs live at the following zoos. Call or write to the zoos to find out about their cheetahs and their plans to preserve cheetahs in the wild. Better yet, go see the cheetahs, person to cat!

Lincoln Park Zoo
2200 N. Cannon Dr.
Chicago, IL 60614
(312) 742-2000

Oklahoma City Zoological Park
2101 NE 50th St.
Oklahoma City, OK 73111-7199
(405) 424-3344

Pittsburgh Zoo
One Wild Place
Pittsburgh, PA 15206
1-800-474-4966

Memphis Zoo
2000 Prentiss Place
Memphis, TN 38112
(901) 276-WILD

WEB SITES

Web sites change frequently, but we believe the following web sites are going to last. You also can use a good search engine, such as **Yahooligans!** [*www.yahooligans.com*] or **Google** [*www.google.com*], to find more information about cheetahs, other big cats around the world, and their homes. Some keywords that will help you are: *cheetahs, savannas, cats, African wildlife, zoo animals,* and *endangered species.*

www.yahooligans.com
Yahooligans! is a great research tool. It has a lot of information and plenty to do. Under Science and Nature, click on Animals and then click on The Big Picture: Animals. From there, you can try Animal Videos, Endangered Animals, Animal Bytes, BBC Animals, or Natural History Notebooks and search for information on cheetahs, savannas, and African wildlife.

library.thinkquest.org/12353
ThinkQuest will show you what other kids are finding out and writing about cheetahs. Just click on African Mammals.

www.super-kids.com
Super-Kids will take you to games and pictures of big cats, along with other information about big cats. Start by clicking on Animals. Then try Africa, Monkeys, Tigers, or Zoos.

www.leopardsetc.com/meet.html
Leopards, Etc. lets you hear big cats. Click on the speaker icon next to each cat name. You can hear all kinds of big cats roaring, growling, rasping, barking, and purring.

www.nationalgeographic.com/features/97/cats/
National Geographic has a really cool game that lets you design the perfect predator.

www.nhm.org/cats/
The Natural History Museum of Los Angeles County has a really great exhibit called *Cats! Mild to Wild.* Click on Biology, and you will find how cats are built, how they use their claws, teeth, legs, and voices — and more!

eelink.net/EndSpp/students-kidssitesandprojects.html
The *EE-Link - Endangered Species* is a great site if you are looking for ideas for homework projects, games, and ways to help save cheetahs and other endangered animals.

www.vrd.org/locator/subject.shtml#science
Do you have more questions about cheetahs? Try *Ask an Expert.* This site has scientists and naturalists who will help you find out whatever you need to know.

GLOSSARY

You can find these words on the pages listed. Reading a word in a sentence helps you understand it even better.

cubs (KUHBZ) — big cats' babies 16, 18, 20

extinct (ex-TINKT) — with none of its kind alive anymore 14

gazelles (guh-ZELZ) — fast, graceful, deerlike animals with long, twisted horns 4, 8, 10

gnus (NUZ) — large African antelopes with drooping beards, tufted tails, and long, curved horns 8

litter (LIT-ur) — a group of cubs born at the same time to the same mother 16

mate (MAYT) — to come together to make babies 16

poaching (POHCH-ing) — the illegal killing of animals 12

predators (PRED-uh-turs) — animals that hunt other animals for food 8, 10, 12, 18

prey (PRAY) — animals that are hunted by other animals for food 6

scavenge (SKAV-uhnj) — to eat the remains of dead animals 10

territory (TER-uh-tor-ee) — area of land that an animal (or group of animals) marks out as its hunting ground 16

warthogs (WORT-hogz) — large African wild pigs with tusks and wartlike knobs on their faces 8

INDEX